WELCOME TO THE BIG CRICKET QUIZ BOOK

Newton Publishing House is a privately run publishing company which cares greatly about the accuracy of its content.

As many questions in this quiz book are subject to change, please email us at **ParagonPublishing23@gmail.com** if you notice any inaccuracies to help us keep our questions as up-to-date as possible.

Happy Quizzing!

CONTENTS

World Cup	4
Cricket Terminology	12
Stadiums	14
ICC World Test Championship	17
IPL	20
The Ashes	28
Champions Trophy	35
Twenty20 World Cup	38
Guess The Player	42
England Cricket	45
General Knowledge	50
Anagram Round	55
Answers	56
World Cup Answers	57
Cricket Terminology Answers	59
Stadiums Answers	60
ICC World Test Championship Answers	61
IPL Answers	62
The Ashes Answers	64
Champions Trophy Answers	66
Twenty20 World Cup Answers	67
Guess The Player Answers	68
England Cricket Answers	69
General Knowledge Answers	70
Anagram Round Answers	71

WORLD CUP

1. Which country did the West Indies beat in the first ODI World Cup final in 1975?
   a. Australia   (b.) India   c. New Zealand   d. England

2. Who has scored the most runs in the ODI World Cup format?
   a. Ricky Ponting   b. Brian Lara   (c.) Sachin Tendulkar   d. Virat Kohli

3. Who has taken the most wickets in the ODI World Cup format?
   (a.) Shane Warne   b. Anil Kumble   c. Glenn McGrath   d. James Anderson

4. Which country hosted the 2003 ODI World Cup?
   (a.) Australia   b. England   c. West Indies   d. South Africa, Zimbabwe and Kenya

5. Which two countries were the joint hosts of the 1992 World Cup?
   a. India & Pakistan   (b.) Australia & New Zealand
   c. India & Sri Lanka   d. South Africa & Zimbabwe

6. Which country will host the 2023 ODI World Cup?
   ~~a. Australia~~   (b.) India   c. South Africa, Zimbabwe and Namibia   d. England

7. Which player was named the Player of the Series in the 2019 ODI World Cup?
   a. Mitchell Starc   b. Kane Williamson   (c.) Joe Root   d. Jofra Archer

8. How many ODI World Cups have Sri Lanka won so far?
   (a.) One   b. Two   c. Three   d. None

9. How many ODI World Cup finals have been held at Lord's Stadium in London?
   a. Two   b. Three   c. Five   (d.) Four

10. In which year did Pakistan lift their only ODI World Cup trophy?
    a. 1987   b. 1996   (c.) 2003   d. 1992

11. Which player has taken the most catches in the ODI World Cup format?
    a. Jonty Rhodes   (b.) Ricky Ponting   c. Yuvraj Singh   d. Kapil Dev

12. Which country holds the record for the lowest score in an ODI World Cup match?
    (a.) Canada   b. Afghanistan   c. Namibia   d. Kenya

13. What is the highest total in an ODI World Cup match?
    a. 398   b. 404   c. 417   (d.) 444

14. Who has won the most consecutive World Cups?
    a. West Indies   b. India   (c.) Australia   d. England

15. In which year did Ireland make its ODI World Cup debut?
    a. 2003   b. 2007   (c.) 2011   d. 2015

16. In which year did Kenya make its ODI World Cup debut?
    (a.) 2003   b. 1996   c. 1999   d. 1992

17. In which version of the ODI World Cup did Bermuda feature?
    a. 2007   b. 2003   c. 2011   (d.) 1999

18. Who won the Man of the Match in the 2011 World Cup Final held in Mumbai?
    a. MS Dhoni   b. Yuvraj Singh   (c.) Sachin Tendulkar   d. Harbhajan Singh

19. Who has scored the most runs in a single ODI World Cup?
    a. Lance Klusener   (b.) Sachin Tendulkar   c. Rohit Sharma   d. Mohammed Shami

20. Which player holds the record for the most runs in a World Cup match?
    a. Martin Guptill   b. Rohit Sharma   c. Sachin Tendulkar   (d.) Chris Gayle

21. Which country was the first to win the cricket World Cup?
    a. West Indies   b. England   (c.) Australia   d. India

22. How many years are there between each World Cup competition?
    a. Two   b. Three   (c.) Four   d. Five

23. How many teams have so far competed in the history of the World Cup competition?
    a. 16   b. 20   (c.) 24   d. 28

24. Which team have won the most matches at the World Cup with 69 victories?
a. India   b. West Indies   c. England   **d. Australia**

25. What has been the best performance by a non full-member team?
a. Netherlands - quarter finals   b. United Arab Emirates - semi finals
c. Kenya - semi finals   d. Canada - final

26. Which of the main test playing nations have lost the most games with 39 defeats?
a. Sri Lanka   **b. West Indies**   c. Pakistan   d. South Africa

27. Which of these umpires appeared in the first World Cup final?
a. Bill Alley   b. David Constant   **c. Arthur Fagg**   d. Dickie Bird

28. Which Australian bowler took the most wickets in the 1975 World Cup?
a. Dennis Lillee   b. Jeff Thomson   c. Gary Gilmour   d. Max Walker

29. How many overs per side were played in the first three competitions before changing to the traditional 50 overs per game?
a. 45   b. 55   c. 60   d. 65

30. In the 1992 semi-final, South Africa needed 22 runs off 13 balls to beat England. What was the target reduced to after a rain interruption?
a. 30 runs off 2 balls   b. 21 runs off 1 ball   c. 25 runs off 3 balls   **d. 19 runs off 8 balls**

31. When Sri Lanka beat Australia to win the 1996 World Cup, where was the final held?
a. Gaddafi Stadium, Lahore, Pakistan   b. Premadasa Stadium, Colombo, Sri Lanka
c. Eden Gardens, Calcutta, India   **d. Feroz Shah Kotla, Delhi, India**

32. How many times had England won the World Cup before 2019?
a. Once   b. Twice   c. Three times   **d. None**

33. What is Sachin Tendulkar's highest score in World Cup competition?
a. 92   b. 112   c. 152   **d. 182**

34. What amazing feat did South African batsman Herschelle Gibbs achieve in a 2007 group game against the Netherlands?
a. Six sixes in an over   b. Six fours in an over
c. A double century   d. Fastest hundred

35. In 2011, India and England tied in a World Cup group game. What totals did both teams achieve?
a. 338   b. 200   c. 175   d. 145

36. What is India's highest total in the World Cup?
a. 373-6   b. 417-6   c. 413-5   d. 350-9

37. What is England's highest total in the World Cup?
a. 417-6   b. 413-5   c. 397-6   d. 386-6

38. What is Pakistan's highest total in the World Cup?
a. 348-8   b. 349   c. 339-6   d. 311

39. Which two West Indian batsman won the Man of the Match awards in the first two World Cups?
a. Clive Lloyd and Viv Richards   b. Gordon Greenidge and Desmond Haynes
c. Brian Lara and Richie Richardson   d. Roy Fredericks and Rohan Kanhai

40. What speed did Pakistan bowler Shoaib Akhtar achieve in a 2003 World Cup game?
a. 120 mph   b. 85 mph   c. 150 mph   d. 100 mph

41. Who was the player of the match for England in the 2019 final?
a. Joe Root   b. Eoin Morgan   c. Ben Stokes   d. Jos Buttler

42. What is Ian Botham's highest score in a World Cup?
a. 84   b. 42   c. 145   d. 53

43. What was unusual about the 2019 World Cup final?
a. Both teams scored over 400 runs   b. It required a super over
c. No result   d. It contained two double centurions

44. What total did both teams score in that final?
a. 241   b. 295   c. 305   d. 211

45. What was the record attendance for the 2015 final between New Zealand and Australia?
a. Over 93,000   b. Over 103,000   c. Over 73,000   d. Over 123,000

46. How much did the West Indian Viv Richards score in the 1979 final?
a. 179   b. 130   c. 138   d. 99

47. Who has the most dismissals by a wicketkeeper in World Cup history?
a. Adam Gilchrist   b. Syed Kirmani   c. Alan Knott   d. Kumar Sangakkara

48. Which team remained undefeated throughout the 2003 and 2007 World Cup campaigns?
a. Australia   c. India   d. Pakistan   c. England

49. Which team made it's one and only appearance in the 1975 competition?
a. USA   b. East Africa   c. Canada   d. Netherlands

50. Having scored the most runs in World Cup history, what is Sachin Tendulkar's amazing average?
a. 56.95   b. 66.95   c. 46.95   d. 76.95

51. What unenviable record does Canada's Nicholas De Groot hold?
a. Three consecutive ducks   b. No runs
c. Most runs conceded   d. Most dropped catches

52. What is the highest partnership in World Cup history?
a. 472   b. 372   c. 272   d. 172

53. What amazing feat did Bermuda's 20-stone Dwayne Leverock achieve in a World Cup match against India in 2007?
a. First ever double century   b. Ten-wicket haul
c. A hat-trick   d. One-handed diving catch

54. Which English ground has hosted the most matches?
a. Lord's   b. Trent Bridge   c. Old Trafford   d. Headingley

55. Which Australian bowler, who holds the record for the most wickets taken, also has the best bowling figures of 7 for 15?
a. Shane Warne   b. Dennis Lillee   c. Brett Lee   d. Glenn McGrath

56. Which West Indian bowler has the best economy rate?
a. Andy Roberts   b. Michael Holding   c. Joel Garner   d. Curtly Ambrose

57. What is Brian Lara's highest score in a World Cup game?
a. 216   b. 156   c. 116   d. 76

58. When was the first Women's World Cup held?
a. 1973   b. 1975   c. 1979   d. 1983

59. When Canada recorded the lowest total in a World Cup match in 2003, what was their final total?
a. 36 all out   b. 40 all out   c. 45 all out   d. 51 all out

60. Which English batsman scored the very first century in 1975?
a. Graham Gooch   b. Geoff Boycott   c. John Edrich   d. Dennis Amiss

61. In the same game, which Indian batsman scored 36 not out in 60 overs of batting?
a. Gundappa Viswanath   b. Bishan Bedi   c. Mohinder Amarnath   d. Sunil Gavaskar

62. The father of England cricketer Derek Pringle played for which team in 1975?
a. England   b. India   c. East Africa   d. Sri Lanka

63. How old was Javed Miandad when he competed in his first World Cup in 1975?
a. 15   b. 17   c. 19   d. 21

64. Which player has captained the most World Cup matches (29) and only has 2 losses?
a. Clive Lloyd   b. Imran Khan   c. MS Dhoni   d. Ricky Ponting

65. When Martin Guptill scored the highest score in a World Cup game, how many runs did he score?
a. 237 not out   b. 257 not out   c. 197 not out   d. 177 not out

66. What are the most runs scored by both teams in one individual game?
a. 788   b. 714   c. 664   d. 608

67. Which cricketer holds the record for the fastest century off only 50 balls?
a. Viv Richards   b. Chris Gayle   c. Sachin Tendulkar   d. Kevin O'Brien

68. Which cricketer has scored the fastest fifty off only 18 balls?
a. Brendon McCullum   b. MS Dhoni   c. Yuvraj Singh   d. Chris Gayle

69. Which company sponsored the first three World Cups?
a. Prudential   b. Norwich Union   c. Red Bull   d. John Player

70. Which batsman has smashed the most sixes in World Cup history?
a. Ricky Ponting   b. Sachin Tendulkar   c. Chris Gayle   d. Viv Richards

71. Which umpire has stood in the most World Cup finals with five?
a. Steve Bucknor   b. Dickie Bird   c. David Shepherd   d. Billy Bowden

72. Which two players have appeared in the most World Cup tournaments with six each?
a. Clive Lloyd and Viv Richards   b. David Gower and Ian Botham
c. Ricky Ponting and Adam Gilchrist   d. Javed Miandad and Sachin Tendulkar

73. What is unusual about England's winning captain Eoin Morgan's appearances in the World Cup?
a. Scored a century in every single game   b. Achieved two hat-tricks
c. Taken most catches in a game   d. Represented two countries

74. Who is the oldest player to appear in a World Cup tournament at the age of 47?
a. Clive Lloyd (West Indies)   b. Alan Knott (England)
c. Nolan Clarke (Netherlands)   d. John Traicos (Zimbabwe)

75. Which team has acheved the highest run chase in a World Cup game with 329?
a. Ireland   b. England   c. Bangladesh   d. India

76. What is Graham Gooch's highest score in a World Cup game?
a. 95   b. 115   c. 145   d. 175

77. Having scored the most runs in World Cup history, which of these other records does Sachin Tendulkar hold?
a. Most runs in a World Cup final   b. Most fifties   c. Most wickets   d. Most catches

78. When did Sachin Tendulkar score his first World Cup century?
a. 1992   b. 1994   c. 1998   d. 1996

79. Which English batsman scored a century against India in the 1987 semi-final?
a. Mike Gatting   b. David Gower   c. Graham Gooch   d. Chris Broad

80. Which Indian bowler took the first ever hat-trick in World Cup history?
a. Kapil Dev   b. Roger Binny   c. Ravi Shastri   d. Chetan Sharma

CRICKET TERMINOLOGY

1. What does the ball do when a bowler bowls a beamer to a batsman?
a. Bounces three times before reaching the batsman
b. Bounces two times before reaching the batsman
c. Bounces zero times before reaching the batsman
d. Bounces once before reaching the batsman

2. What does the term LBW stand for?
a. Limping beside wicket   b. Leg beside wicket
c. Limping before wicket   d. Leg before wicket

3. How many official ways can you be dismissed in cricket?
a. Eight   b. Ten   c. Twelve   d. Fourteen

4. Which country uses the term 'bosie' for a googly delivery?
a. Australia   b. South Africa   c. New Zealand   d. England

5. Who usually bowls a googly?
a. Fast bowler   b. Medium pace bowler   c. Off-spinner   d. Leg-spinner

6. When was 'Hawk-Eye' first introduced into international cricket?
a. 1999   b. 2001   c. 2003   d. 2005

7. When was the 'powerplay' first used in one-day international cricket?
a. 2002   b. 2003   c. 2004   d. 2005

8. The Marylebone Cricket Club, based in London, is better known by what three letter name?
a. MCU   b. MCM   c. MCC   d. MUC

9. A 'Nelson' is usually which one of these scores?
a. 11   b. 111   c. 222   d. 22

10. Can you be dismissed off a no-ball?
a. Yes - by hit wicket   b. Yes - by lbw
c. Yes - by being stumped   d. Yes - by being run out

11. A batsman being dismissed for a 'pair' applies to which of these?
a. Scoring a hundred in each innings   b. Scoring one run in each innings
c. Scoring zero in both innings   d. Scoring a fifty in both innings

12. Which English captain got dismissed by playing a 'reverse sweep' in the 1987 World Cup final?
a. Mike Gatting   b. Allan Lamb   c. Ian Botham   d. Graham Gooch

13. The rarely used term 'rock' is used for which piece of cricketing equipment?
a. Ball   b. Bat   c. Pads   d. Stumps

14. Which part of the body does the 'box' protect?
a. Head   b. Legs   c. Arms   d. Abdominal region

15. What other term is used when a batsman hits a four or a six?
a. Bye   b. Boundary   c. Belter   d. Beamer

16. A 'yorker' is usually aimed at the batsman's....?
a. Head   b. Body   c. Legs   d. Toes

17. The term 'in the V' refers to which areas of the field?
a. Between third man and wicket keeper   b. Between bowler and the slips
c. Between point and short leg   d. Between mid-on and mid-off

18. A cricketer who just misses out on playing in the starting eleven is known as what?
a. First man   b. Second man   c. Last man   d. Twelfth man

19. A shortened version of the game with different scoring systems, a predecessor to twenty20 cricket, and introduced in the 1990s, was called by what name?
a. Cricket Thrillers   b. Cricket Max   c. Cricket Smash   d. Cricket Bash

20. 'Cow corner' refers to what?
a. Batting stroke   b. Type of delivery   c. Fielding position   d. Type of dismissal

STADIUMS

1. Which cricket ground currently holds the record for the highest capacity, seating over 130,000 people?
a. Melbourne Cricket Ground, Melbourne, Australia
b. Eden Park, Auckland, New Zealand
c. The Oval, London, England
d. Narendra Modi Stadium, Ahmedabad, India

2. Which other cricket ground currently has over a 100,000 capacity?
a. Eden Gardens, Kolkata, India
b. Perth Stadium, Perth, Australia
c. Melbourne Cricket Ground, Melbourne, Australia
d. Barabati Stadium, Cuttack, India

3. Which Indian cricket ground previously had an estimated 100,000 attendance in international matches?
a. Wankhede Stadium, Mumbai
b. Eden Gardens, Kolkata
c. Green Park Stadium, Kanpur
d. Rajiv Gandhi International Cricket Stadium, Hyderabad

4. Which two countries hold the most grounds with high attendance capabilities in world cricket?
a. England and South Africa   b. Pakistan and Sri Lanka
c. West Indies and New Zealand   d. Australia and India

5. Which ground hosted the first ever test match in England in 1880?
a. Lord's   b. The Oval   c. Old Trafford   d. Trent Bridge

6. How many different grounds have hosted international test match cricket so far?
a. 102   b. 112   c. 121   d. 134

7. Which UK ground became the 100th different venue to be used for test match cricket in 2009?
a. Grace Road, Leicester   b. Rose Bowl, Southampton
c. Riverside Ground, Chester-le-Street   d. Sophia Gardens, Cardiff

8. Buffalo Park, Newlands, and Kingsmead are grounds in which country?
a. England   b. West Indies   c. Australia   d. South Africa

9. Which of these non-test match playing countries have hosted an international five day game?
a. Kenya   b. Canada   c. Netherlands   d. UAE

10. In which city was the first official international cricket match between the United States and Canada held?
a. Washington DC   b. New York   c. Philadelphia   d. Orlando

11. Which country has hosted international matches in the most number of grounds?
a. India   b. England   c. Australia   d. Pakistan

12. Wankhede, Brabourne, and Dr DY Patil Sports Academy are cricket stadiums situated in which city?
a. Mumbai, India   b. London, England
c. Johannesburg, South Africa   d. Calcutta, India

13. Which city hosted the first ever 'test' match?
a. Melbourne, Australia   b. Johannesburg, South Africa
c. London, England   d. Mumbai, India

14. On which ground did Sri Lanka score a test record 952 for 6 playing India?
a. Galle International Stadium, Galle   b. Sinhalese Sports Club Ground, Colombo
c. Asgiriya Stadium, Kandy   d. R. Premadasa Stadium, Colombo

15. At which West Indian venue did Brian Lara score a record 400 runs against England?
a. St. John's, Antigua   b. Bridgetown, Barbados
c. Kingston, Jamaica   d. Georgetown, Guyana

16. In which country are the Gabba, the WACA, and the SCG situated?
a. South Africa   b. West Indies   c. Australia   d. England

17. Apart from cricket, on which of these grounds does the sport of Australian Rules Football also take place?
a. Docklands, Melbourne   b. Old Trafford, Manchester
c. Kingsmead, Durban   d. Queens Sports Club, Bulawayo

18. In which two main cities has test cricket taken place in Zimbabwe?
a. Harare and Mutare   b. Gweru and Bulawayo
c. Bulawayo and Kwekwe   d. Harare and Bulawayo

19. Where do the English county of Leicestershire play their home games?
a. Trent Bridge   b. Taunton   c. Grace Road   d. Headingley

20. Lord's cricket ground is home to which English county?
a. Surrey   b. Middlesex   c. Kent   d. Essex

ICC WORLD TEST CHAMPIONSHIP

1. Who is eligible to compete in the World Test Championship?
a. All eligible test playing nations   b. All international teams
c. All club teams   d. All twenty20 teams

2. When was the first tournament due to take place?
a. 2009   b. 2011   c. 2013   d. 2015

3. Which team won the first edition of the Championship?
a. South Africa   b. England   c. New Zealand   d. Australia

4. Who did they beat in the final?
a. West Indies   b. India   c. Australia   d. Pakistan

5. Which Australian has scored the most centuries in one tournament?
a. David Warner   b. Marnus Labuschagne   c. Steve Smith   d. Usman Khawaja

6. Which Australian batsman has the current highest score of 335 not out?
a. David Warner   b. Marnus Labuschagne   c. Steve Smith   d. Usman Khawaja

7. Which team recorded the present lowest total of 36 against Australia?
a. Pakistan   b. Sri Lanka   c. West Indies   d. India

8. Which New Zealand bowler recently recorded the best figures in the competition by taking all ten wickets in an innings?
a. Kyle Jamieson   b. Tim Southee   c. Ajaz Patel   d. Trent Boult

9. Which English ground hosted the final in 2021?
a. The Oval   b. Edgbaston   c. Lord's   d. Rose Bowl

10. Which competition was the first championship scheduled to replace?
a. ICC Champions Trophy   b. The Ashes   c. World Twenty20   d. IPL

11. Which former New Zealand batsman was the inspiration behind the new tournament?
a. Glenn Turner   b. John Reid   c. Bruce Edgar   d. Martin Crowe

12. How many test playing nations were supposed to take part in the first tournament in 2013?
a. Five   b. Ten   c. Fifteen   d. Twenty

13. When the 2017 championship was also cancelled, which tournament took place instead?
a. The World Cup   b. World Twenty20   c. T10   d. ICC Champions Trophy

14. When the championship finally started in 2019, which test series did it begin with?
a. Border-Gavaskar Trophy   b. The Ashes   c. The Wisden Trophy   d. Asia Cup

15. Where was the first game played?
a. Edgbaston, Birmingham   b. Old Trafford, Manchester
c. The Gabba, Brisbane   d. SCG, Sydney

16. What was the result at the end of the series?
a. England win   b. Australia win   c. Tied   d. No Result

17. Who finished top of the 2019/21 League table?
a. New Zealand   b. England   c. India   d. Australia

18. Which three full member nations did not compete in this competition due to their low ranking?
a. Sri Lanka, Pakistan, and Zimbabwe   b. West Indies, Scotland, and UAE
c. England, South Africa, and Ireland   d. Afghanistan, Ireland, and Zimbabwe

19. Which Indian bowler took the most wickets in this tournament with 71 dismissals?
a. Ravichandran Ashwin   b. Virat Kohli   c. Mohammed Shami   d. Jasprit Bumrah

20. How was the result of the 2021 final eventually resolved despite rain?
a. Reserve day used   b. Toss of coin   c. Boundary count   d. 50-over match

21. What did Indian captain Virat Kohli suggest for future test championships?
a. 50-over matches   b. Timeless tests   c. No reserve days   d. Best-of-three series

22. How much did the winning team collect?
a. 0.5 million US dollars   b. 1.6 million US dollars
c. 3.2 million US dollars   d. 5 million US dollars

23. Which team collected the least amount of points, having also played the least number of games, after the league stage?
a. South Africa   b. West Indies   c. Bangladesh   d. Zimbabwe

24. Over which time period is the next championship scheduled?
a. 2023-25   b. 2020-24   c. 2021-23   d. 2025-27

25. How many points will be awarded to each team for a win in this championship?
a. 8   b. 12   c. 16   d. 20

26. Who presently holds the record for the most runs in recent matches, and overall in the championship history?
a. KL Rahul (India)   b. Tom Latham (New Zealand)
c. Steve Smith (Australia)   d. Joe Root (England)

27. What does ICC stand for?
a. International Cricket Committee   b. International Cricket Council
c. International Cricket Community   d. International Competition Company

28. Where did England finish in the 2019/21 League table?
a. Second   b. Fourth   c. Third   d. Fifth

29. Which England bowler has taken the most wickets to date for his country?
a. James Anderson   b. Matthew Hoggard   c. Ben Stokes   d. Stuart Broad

30. Which team has played the most matches to date in the history of the championship, but also suffered the most defeats?
a. England   b. India   c. Australia   d. West Indies

IPL

1. When was the first version of the IPL held?
a. 2001   b. 2008   c. 2015   d. 2019

2. What does the IPL stand for?
a. Indian Premier League   b. Indian Players League
c. International Pro League   d. Indian Pro League

3. Who won the inaugural IPL tournament?
a. Chennai Super Kings   b. Deccan Chargers
c. Mumbai Indians   d. Rajasthan Royals

4. Who scored an amazing 158 not out in the very first game of the IPL 2008?
a. Chris Gayle   b. Brendon McCullum   c. Virat Kohli   d. AB de Villiers

5. Which team finished top of the league table in the very first IPL tournament?
a. Delhi Daredevils   b. Kolkata Knight Riders   c. Rajasthan Royals   d. Pune Warriors

6. Who hit the winning runs in the inaugural IPL final in 2008?
a. Yusuf Pathan   b. Shane Warne   c. Shane Watson   d. Sohail Tanvir

7. Which team has won the IPL the greatest number of times?
a. Mumbai Indians   b. Chennai Super Kings
c. Punjab Kings/Kings XI Punjab   d. Deccan Chargers

8. Which team won the most recent IPL tournament in 2021?
a. Chennai Super Kings   b. Mumbai Indians
c. Kolkata Knight Riders   d. Delhi Capitals

9. Which team came second in the 2021 IPL?
a. Delhi Capitals   b. Mumbai Indians
c. Royal Challengers Bangalore   d. Kolkata Knight Riders

10. Which Indian batsman has scored the most runs in IPL history?
a. KL Rahul   b. Virat Kohli   c. Sachin Tendulkar   d. Rohit Sharma

11. Which IPL team does Virat Kohli play for?
a. Delhi Capitals　　　　　b. Punjab Kings
c. Royal Challengers Bangalore　d. Chennai Super Kings

12. Which non-Indian batsman has scored the most runs in the IPL?
a. Chris Gayle　b. AB de Villiers　c. Jacques Kallis　d. David Warner

13. Which Indian batsman has the best average in the IPL, having played over 90 games?
a. Virat Kohli　b. KL Rahul　c. Virender Sehwag　d. Rohit Sharma

14. Which West Indian batsman has hit the most sixes in the history of the IPL, over a 100 ahead of his next best challenger?
a. Chris Gayle　b. Marlon Samuels　c. Kieron Pollard　d. Andre Russell

15. Which South African batsman is second on the list of batsman with most sixes in IPL history?
a. Jonty Rhodes　b. Graeme Smith　c. Hashim Amla　d. AB de Villiers

16. Which batsman has struck the most sixes in an individual IPL innings with 17?
a. AB de Villiers　b. Yusuf Pathan　c. Chris Morris　d. Chris Gayle

17. What record IPL score did Chris Gayle achieve in the innings where he scored 17 sixes?
a. 130 not out　b. 158 not out　c. 175 not out　d. 215 not out

18. Which Sri Lankan bowler has taken the most wickets in the IPL, with an average of 19.79?
a. Chaminda Vaas　　b. Muttiah Muralitharan
c. Farveez Maharoof　d. Lasith Malinga

19. Which bowler achieved the best IPL bowling figures whilst playing for Mumbai Indians against Sunrisers Hyderabad in 2019, with 6 for 12?
a. Harbhajan Singh　b. Trent Boult　c. Jasprit Bumrah　d. Alzarri Joseph

20. How many bowlers have taken six wickets in an innings in the IPL?
a. One　b. Three　c. Seven　d. Nine

21. Which all-rounder took 32 wickets for Chennai Super Kings in the 2013 IPL tournament?
a. Ravindra Jadeja   b. Dwayne Bravo   c. Kieran Pollard   d. Suresh Raina

22. Which two Indian wicket-keepers have taken over a 100 dismissals in the IPL?
a. MS Dhoni & Dinesh Karthik   b. Rishabh Pant & Parthiv Patel
c. Wriddhiman Saha & Parthiv Patel   d. Rishabh Pant & MS Dhoni

23. Who is the only player to have taken over 100 catches in the IPL?
a. AB de Villiers   b. Suresh Raina   c. Ricky Ponting   d. Brendon McCullum

24. Which pair of batsmen have the highest partnership records in the IPL?
a. Chris Gayle & Virat Kohli   b. AB de Villiers & Virat Kohli
c. Lendl Simmons & Parthiv Patel   d. Jonny Bairstow & David Warner

25. Who is the only captain to have skippered in over 200 IPL matches?
a. Virat Kohli   b. Gautam Gambhir   c. Rohit Sharma   d. MS Dhoni

26. Which is the only defunct team to have won the IPL title?
a. Deccan Chargers   b. Pune Warriors   c. Gujarat Lions   d. Rising Pune Supergiants

27. How many times have Kolkata Knight Riders won the IPL title?
a. Never   b. Two   c. Four   d. Six

28. Which three teams have competed in every single edition of the IPL, but never won the title?
a. Mumbai Indians, Chennai Super Kings & Kolkata Knight Riders
b. Chennai Super Kings, Kolkata Knight Riders & Rajasthan Royals
c. Mumbai Indians, Delhi Capitals & Royal Challengers Bangalore
d. Royal Challengers Bangalore, Delhi Capitals & Punjab Kings

29. Apart from India, in which two countries has the IPL tournament taken place?
a. UAE & South Africa   b. UAE & Australia
c. West Indies & South Africa   d. South Africa & Australia

30. Which team has finished runners-up five times in the IPL tournament?
a. Chennai Super Kings   b. Mumbai Indians   c. Delhi Capitals   d. Rajasthan Royals

31. In the IPL, what is the Orange Cap?
a. Awarded to the player with most wickets
b. Awarded to the player with most catches
c. Awarded to the player with most run outs
d. Awarded to the player with most runs

32. In the IPL, what is the Purple Cap?
a. Awarded to the player with most wickets
b. Awarded to the player with most catches
c. Awarded to the player with most run outs
d. Awarded to the player with most runs

33. Dwayne Bravo and which other Indian player have won the IPL Purple Cap on two separate occasions?
a. Harbhajan Singh   b. Jasprit Bumrah
c. Bhuvneshwar Kumar   d. Mohammed Shami

34. In which year did Sachin Tendulkar win the IPL Man of the Tournament award?
a. 2008   b. 2010   c. 2012   d. 2014

35. How many times has Sachin Tendulkar won the IPL player of the match award in a final?
a. Two times   b. Three times   c. Once   d. None

36. Which Indian keeper won the IPL Emerging Player award in 2018?
a. Dinesh Karthik   b. Parthiv Patel   c. Rishabh Pant   d. Sanju Samson

37. In which year did Indian batsman Rohit Sharma win IPL Emerging Player award?
a. 2008   b. 2009   c. 2010   d. 2011

38. Which team has won the IPL Fair Play award on seven different occasions?
a. Kolkata Knight Riders   b. Mumbai Indians
c. Royal Challengers Bangalore   d. Chennai Super Kings

39. Have RCB or KKR ever won this IPL Fair Play award?
a. Yes – once   b. Yes – three times   c. No – never   d. Yes – two times

40. Which team has played the greatest number of games in the IPL, having competed in every single version?
a. Delhi Capitals   b. Mumbai Indians   c. Punjab Kings   d. Rajasthan Royals

41. Which team has the highest win record percentage in IPL history?
a. Delhi Capitals   b. Mumbai Indians   c. Punjab Kings   d. Chennai Super Kings

42. How many times have teams won by just one run in IPL history?
a. Eleven times   b. Nine times   c. Fifteen times   d. Seven times

43. Which team achieved the highest successful run chase in the 2020 IPL tournament?
a. Rajasthan Royals   b. Mumbai Indians   c. Kolkata Knight Riders   d. Punjab Kings

44. Which team holds the two highest totals record in the IPL?
a. Rajasthan Royals   b. Mumbai Indians
c. Royal Challengers Bangalore   d. Punjab Kings

45. Which unenviable record does Royal Challengers Bangalore hold in the IPL?
a. Most defeats   b. Lowest team total
c. Most ducks in an innings   d. No boundaries in an innings

46. Who is the only batsman to have hit over 50 half-centuries in the IPL?
a. Virat Kohli   b. Chris Gayle   c. AB de Villiers   d. David Warner

47. In 2018, which Indian batsman hit the fastest fifty in IPL history?
a. Ravindra Jadeja   b. Yusuf Pathan   c. Shreyas Iyer   d. KL Rahul

48. Which West Indian batsman holds the record for the fastest century in the history of the IPL?
a. Brian Lara   b. Chris Gayle   c. Andre Russell   d. Shimron Hetmyer

49. Which South African player has the highest strike rate in an innings, of 422.22, when scoring 38 not out off nine balls in a 2017 IPL match?
a. AB de Villiers   b. Hashim Amla   c. Albie Morkel   d. Chris Morris

50. Which current South African bowler has the best career strike rate in the IPL?
a. Chris Morris   b. Kagiso Rabada   c. Lungi Ngidi   d. Imran Tahir

51. Which West Indian bowler has taken the most four-wicket (8 over) hauls in the IPL?
a. Sunil Narine   b. Andre Russell   c. Dwayne Bravo   d. Fidel Edwards

52. Which bowler conceded a record 70 runs playing for Sunrisers Hyderabad against RCB in the 2018 IPL?
a. Rashid Khan   b. Basil Thampi   c. Ishant Sharma   d. Shakib Al Hasan

53. Who was the first bowler to take a hat-trick in the IPL?
a. Lasith Malinga   b. Lakshmipathy Balaji   c. Irfan Pathan   d. Shane Warne

54. Which Indian spinner is the only player to have taken three hat-tricks in IPL history?
a. Harbhajan Singh   b. Harshal Patel   c. Pragyan Ojha   d. Amit Mishra

55. Who was the last player to take a hat-trick in the 2021 IPL tournament?
a. Dwayne Bravo   b. Ravindra Jadeja   c. Harshal Patel   d. Ravichandran Ashwin

56. Which Indian keeper has achieved the most stumpings in IPL history?
a. MS Dhoni   b. Parthiv Patel   c. Dinesh Karthik   d. Rishabh Pant

57. Who is the only fielder to have taken five catches in an innings in an IPL match?
a. Brendon McCullum   b. Ricky Ponting   c. Rahul Dravid   d. Mohammad Nabi

58. Which team had ten consecutive wins between the 2014 & 2015 IPL tournaments?
a. Chennai Super Kings   b. Kings XI Punjab
c. Delhi Capitals   d. Kolkata Knight Riders

59. Which South African has won the most IPL Man of the Match awards?
a. Graeme Smith   b. Lance Klusener   c. AB de Villiers   d. Dale Steyn

60. Which two Mumbai Indians batsmen achieved a 100-run partnership for the seventh wicket in the 2015 IPL?
a. Harbhajan Singh & Kieron Pollard   b. Harbhajan Singh & Lasith Malinga
c. Harbhajan Singh & Jagadeesha Suchith   d. Harbhajan Singh & Rohit Sharma

61. Which Indian umpire has officiated the most number of times in the IPL with 131 games?
a. Nitin Menon   b. Anil Chaudhary   c. Sundaram Ravi   d. Sudhir Asnani

62. Which Sri Lankan umpire is third on the list of most IPL appearances?
a. Kumar Sangakkara   b. Kumar Dharmasena   c. BC Cooray   d. Asoka de Silva

63. Bollywood actor Shah Rukh Khan co-owns which IPL franchise?
a. Kolkata Knight Riders   b. Mumbai Indians
c. Chennai Super Kings   d. Royal Challengers Bangalore

64. Which Bollywood actress is one of the joint owners of Punjab Kings/Kings XI Punjab in the IPL?
a. Priyanka Chopra   b. Hema Malini   c. Preity Zinta   d. Lara Dutta

65. Which Indian spinner is the current coach of IPL side Punjab Kings?
a. Harbhajan Singh   b. Ravi Shastri   c. Pragyan Ojha   d. Anil Kumble

66. Which former Sri Lankan batsman is the current head coach of IPL team Mumbai Indians?
a. Kumar Sangakkara   b. Sanath Jayasuriya
c. Mahela Jayawardene   d. Arjuna Ranatunga

67. Who did Harbhajan Singh allegedly slap in the face in the 2008 IPL?
a. S Sreesanth   b. Ishant Sharma   c. Yusuf Pathan   d. Amit Mishra

68. In which season did the BCCI suspend the IPL chairman4 Lalit Modi?
a. 2008   b. 2012   c. 2016   d. 2010

69. What was Indian player Sreesanth accused of in the 2013 IPL tournament?
a. Ball tampering   b. Using a metal bat   c. Spot-fixing   d. Not turning up to play

70. In which month did the 2021 season resume after being suspended due to the Covid outbreak in India?
a. September 2021   b. October 2021   c. August 2021   d. November 2021

71. How many centuries were scored in the only IPL competition in South Africa in 2009?
a. None   b. Two   c. Six   d. Eight

72. IPL side Royal Challengers Bangalore are named after what type of brand?
a. Alcohol   b. Soft Drinks   c. Engineering   d. Toys

73. Eden Gardens is the home ground of which IPL team?
a. Mumbai Indians   b. Sunrisers Hyderabad
c. Delhi Capitals   d. Kolkata Knight Riders

74. What reason was given for the IPL team Delhi Daredevils changing their name to Delhi Capitals?
a. Being capital of India   b. No reason
c. Change in sponsorship   d. For investment purposes

75. After Deccan Chargers were banned, which team now represents the city of Hyderabad in the IPL?
a. Indians   b. Super Kings   c. Sunrisers   d. Royals

76. How many centuries did Sachin Tendulkar score in the IPL?
a. None   b. Two   c. Five   d. One

77. How many Player of the Match awards did Sachin Tendulkar win in the IPL?
a. None   b. Two   c. Five   d. Eight

78. Which team has won the most number of games in the IPL?
a. Kolkata Knight Riders   b. Mumbai Indians
c. Chennai Super Kings   c. Royal Challengers Bangalore

79 After CSK, which team did MS Dhoni play for in the IPL?
a. Gujarat Lions   b. Pune Warriors   c. Rising Pune Supergiants   d. Delhi Capitals

80. After Mumbai Indians, which IPL team did Harbhajan Singh play for?
a. Kolkata Knight Riders   b. Rajasthan Royals
c. Chennai Super Kings   d. Royal Challengers Bangalore

THE ASHES

1. Which two cricket teams compete in the Ashes?
a. Australia & England   b. India & England
c. West Indies & India   d. Australia & South Africa

2. In which decade was the first ever Ashes test match held?
a. 1850s   b. 1870s   c. 1860s   d. 1880s

3. Which batsman faced the first delivery in the first ever test match?
a. Charles Bannerman   b. Tom Garrett   c. Billy Murdoch   d. WG Grace

4. Which English player scored his country's first 50 in test cricket?
a. Harry Jupp   b. WG Grace   c. Edward Grace   d. Tom Emmett

5. What does the 'Ashes' symbolise in test cricket?
a. A burnt bail   b. A burnt bat   c. A burnt cap   d. A burnt ball

6. Who was the first English test match captain?
a. Douglas Jardine   b. Ivo Bligh   c. WG Grace   d. James Lillywhite

7. How many centuries did Australian Don Bradman score against England in tests?
a. 10   b. 12   c. 19   d. 22

8. How many of Don Bradman's test match centuries were converted into double centuries and over when playing against England?
a. 6   b. 8   c. 4   d. 11

9. What was the score that Australia won by to win the 2021-22 Ashes series?
a. 5-0   b. 4-1   c. 3-1   d. 4-0

10. What was so 'invincible' about the 1948 Australian cricket team in England?
a. Unbeaten on tour   b. Lost every match
c. Totalled 600 in every game   d. Won every match by an innings

11. What amazing average did Don Bradman end up with against England in test matches?
a. 110.14   b. 99.14   c. 69.14   d. 89.78

12. Which English test batsman averaged over 160 at the Sydney cricket ground?
a. Len Hutton   b. Jack Hobbs   c. Wally Hammond   d. Geoff Boycott

13. Where is the original Ashes Urn now kept?
a. Melbourne Cricket Ground   b. Lord's Cricket Ground   c. The Oval   d. ICC Office

14. How many 'Ashes' test matches have been played so far as of February 2022?
a. 140   b. 240   c. 340   d. 440

15. Which team has won the most Ashes test series?
a. England   b. All level   c. MCC   d. Australia

16. In which series did the 'Ashes' legend begin?
a. 1877   b. 1882/83   c. 1902   d. 1922/23

17. Which Australian bowler helped his team to victory over the English in an 1882 test match with 14 wickets at the Oval?
a. Fred Spofforth   b. Clarrie Grimmett   c. Tom Garrett   d. George Giffen

18. What is now presented to the winning team of each Ashes series?
a. The Urn   b. The Ashes Trophy   c. A Cup   d. Replica Ball

19. Who scored three centuries for England in the 1986/87 test series against Australia?
a. David Gower   b. Chris Broad   c. Allan Lamb   d. Mike Gatting

20. Who was England batsman Chris Broad's opening partner in the 1986/87 test series against Australia?
a. David Gower   b. Bill Athey   c. Graham Gooch   d. Allan Lamb

21. Who captained the England test team in the 1986/87 series against Australia?
a. David Gower   b. Ian Botham   c. Allan Lamb   d. Mike Gatting

22. Who was the Australian captain in the 1986/87 Ashes series against England?
a. Kim Hughes   b. Dean Jones   c. Allan Border   d. David Boon

23. At which venue did England win a test match after being odds of 500-1 against in 1981?
a. Headingley   b. Trent Bridge   c. Edgbaston   d. The Oval

24. At which venue did Ian Botham take 5 wickets for 1 run during the 1981 Ashes?
a. Trent Bridge   b. Old Trafford   c. Edgbaston   d. The Oval

25. Which Australian bowler played his last 'Ashes' test in 1981?
a. Terry Alderman   b. Jeff Thomson   c. Max Walker   d. Dennis Lillee

26. Which Australian wicket-keeper took the most catches off the bowling of team mate Dennis Lillee in test matches?
a. Rod Marsh   b. Wally Grout   c. Steve Rixon   d. Alan Knott

27. Who captained England during the 'Bodyline' test series?
a. Wally Hammond   b. Herbert Sutcliffe   c. Jack Hobbs   d. Douglas Jardine

28. At which batsman was the 'Bodyline' ploy mainly aimed at?
a. Bill Ponsford   b. Warwick Armstrong   c. Don Bradman   d. Stan McCabe

29. Which England bowler took the most wickets during the 1932/33 Bodyline test series?
a. Bill Voce   b. Harold Larwood   c. Gubby Allen   d. Hedley Verity

30. Where did England bowler Harold Larwood eventually live after retirement?
a. England   b. Australia   c. South Africa   d. Kenya

31. What was Don Bradman's highest test score in the 1932/33 Bodyline series against England?
a. 167   b. 93   c. 103   d. 142

32. What was the highest test score record held by Don Bradman?
a. 289   b. 247   c. 334   d. 371

33. Who eventually broke Don Bradman's highest test score record in 1938?
a. Jack Hobbs   b. Wally Hammond   c. Denis Compton   d. Len Hutton

34. How much did Len Hutton score in a 1938 Ashes test match at The Oval?
a. 344   b. 364   c. 384   d. 404

35. How long did Len Hutton bat for during his score of 364 in a 1938 Ashes test?
a. Over 6 hours   b. Over 10 hours   c. Over 13 hours   d. Over 16 hours

36. What is Ian Botham's highest score in an Ashes test match?
a. 89   b. 109   c. 129   d. 149

37. Which Australian captain was instrumental in winning the Ashes back in 1989?
a. Allan Border   b. Mark Taylor   c. Kim Hughes   d. Steve Waugh

38. Which player, with the last name Taylor, played his first Ashes series in 1989?
a. Peter   b. Mark   c. Bob   d. Michael

39. How many runs did this Taylor score in his first Ashes series?
a. 639   b. 739   c. 839   d. 939

40. Who was Australia's leading bowler in the 1985 Ashes test series against England?
a. Geoff Lawson   b. Terry Alderman   c. Carl Rackemann   d. Craig McDermott

41. Who topped the Aussie bowling in the 1981 and 1989 Ashes test series?
a. Geoff Lawson   b. Terry Alderman   c. Carl Rackemann   d. Craig McDermott

42. Who took the famous figures of 8 for 43 in a 1981 Ashes test?
a. Ian Botham   b. Graham Gooch   c. Bob Willis   d. Graham Dilley

43. The man of the series in the 2021/22 Ashes series was given to which player?
a. Joe Root   b. Mitchell Starc   c. Pat Cummins   d. Travis Head

44. What score did England achieve in the 1978/79 tour to Australia?
a. 1-0 series win   b. 2-1 series win   c. 3-0 series loss   d. 5-1 series win

45. How many runs did Graham Gooch score in his first Ashes test?
a. 0   b. 50   c. 100   d. 200

46. Who was the man of the series for England in the 2005 Ashes triumph?
a. Andrew Strauss   b. Michael Vaughan   c. Simon Jones   d. Andrew Flintoff

47. Who did Steve Harmison dismiss to help England win the Edgbaston test by two runs during the 2005 Ashes series?
a. Shane Warne   b. Michael Kasprowicz   c. Adam Gilchrist   d. Damien Martyn

48. Where did England achieve a three-run win in a 1982 overseas test?
a. Adelaide   b. Sydney   c. Perth   d. Melbourne

49. What was the eventual score in the 1982/83 Ashes series?
a. England 2-1   b. Australia 2-1   c. 0-0   d. 3-3

50. What feat did English batsman Reg 'Tip' Foster achieve in a 1903/04 test match?
a. Pair on debut   b. Hundred on debut
c. Double-hundred on debut   d. Run out twice

51. Which test record did England's Reg 'Tip' Foster create in his innings of 287 against Australia in 1903/04?
a. Highest Individual score in tests   b. Fastest 50 in tests
c. Fastest 100   d. Fastest 200

52. What totals did both teams achieve in a 1964 test match in Manchester, England?
a. 656 & 611   b. 456 & 411   c. 156 & 111   d. 856 & 811

53. Who top scored for Australia in the total of 656 against England in a 1964 test match?
a. Bill Lawry   b. Lindsay Hassett   c. Bobby Simpson   d. Richie Benaud

54. Who top scored for England in a 1964 test match against Australia when his team totalled 611?
a. Geoff Boycott   b. Ken Barrington   c. Denis Compton   d. John Edrich

55. How many wickets did Australian's Dennis Lillee and Jeff Thomson share in the 1974/75 test series against England?
a. 28   b. 48   c. 58   d. 88

56. For how many was Ian Botham dismissed for in the second innings of the 1981 Ashes test at Lord's?
a. Duck   b. 50   c. 100   d. 150

57. How many did Botham score in his first innings after losing the captaincy in the same series?
a. Duck   b. 50   c. 100   d. 150

58. Which pop legend hosted parties for the England team down under in Australia during the 1986/87 series?
a. Elton John   b. David Bowie   c. Stevie Wonder   d. Paul Weller

59. Who scored three hundreds in the 1985 Ashes series?
a. David Gower   b. Allan Border   c. Tim Robinson   d. Mike Gatting

60. Who sponsored the 2021/22 Ashes series in Australia?
a. Specsavers   b. Prudential   c. Vodafone   d. Toyota

61. Who sponsored the 2005 Ashes series?
a. Specsavers   b. Prudential   c. Npower   d. Cornhill

62. Which England bowler took all ten wickets in an innings in a 1956 test match?
a. Tony Lock   b. Fred Trueman   c. Jim Laker   d. Brian Statham

63. How many wickets did Jim Laker take in a 1956 test match against Australia that broke all wicket taking records?
a. 20   b. 19   c. 15   d. 10

64. After how many years did England win back the Ashes when they triumphed in 1953?
a. 10 years   b. 5 years   c. 20 years   d. 25 years

65. Who was instrumental in England's Ashes test series win in 1953 with 39 wickets?
a. Jim Laker   b. Fred Trueman   c. Trevor Bailey   d. Alec Bedser

66. Who was the England test captain in the 1953 Ashes series?
a. Len Hutton   b. Fred Trueman   c. Denis Compton   d. Peter May

67. For how many series did Allan Border captain his Australian side to Ashes victory?
a. Once   b. Twice   c. Three times   d. Four times

68. When was the last time England held the Ashes?
a. 2000   b. 2005   c. 2010   d. 2015

69. Which ground has hosted the most Ashes tests?
a. Lord's   b. Sydney   c. Melbourne   d. The Oval

70. What is England's Joe Root's highest score in an Ashes test match?
a. 160   b. 230   c. 180   d. 200

71. Australian batsman Marnus Labuschagne has played for which English county?
a. Glamorgan   b. Somerset   c. Kent   d. Surrey

72. Adam Gilchrist's fastest hundred against England was completed in how many balls?
a. 57   b. 87   c. 107   d. 127

73. Australian Bob Cowper batted for how many minutes when he scored 307 against England in a 1966 test?
a. 1127   b. 527   c. 727   d. 927

74. How long did Bobby Simpson's 311 take in a 1964 test match?
a. 562 minutes   b. 762 minutes   c. 962 minutes   d. 1062 minutes

75. How many wickets did Andrew Flintoff take in the 2005 Ashes series?
a. 14   b. 24   c. 34   d. 44

76. Who was the England coach at the time of the 2005 Ashes win?
a. Andy Flower   b. Tom Moody   c. Trevor Penney   d. Duncan Fletcher

77. Who has scored the most runs in an Ashes series with 974 runs?
a. Don Bradman   b. Wally Hammond   c. Alastair Cook   d. Steve Smith

78. Who has taken the most wickets, with 46, in an Ashes test series?
a. Jim Laker   b. Terry Alderman   c. Dennis Lillee   d. Shane Warne

79. With 54, who has taken the most catches in Ashes test matches?
a. Ian Botham   b. Greg Chappell   c. Mark Taylor   d. Mark Waugh

80. Which English umpire has stood in the most Ashes tests?
a. Ken Palmer   b. David Shepherd   c. Dickie Bird   d. Frank Chester

CHAMPIONS TROPHY

1. The Champions Trophy is played over what format?
a. 50 overs   b. 20 overs   c. Five days   d. 10 overs

2. In which year was the first Champions Trophy tournament held?
a. 1990   b. 1994   c. 1998   d. 2003

3. In which country was the first Champions Trophy held?
a. Sri Lanka   b. Pakistan   c. Bangladesh   d. England

4. Which South African was the player of the tournament with the most wickets in the very first Champions Trophy?
a. Shaun Pollock   b. Lance Klusener   c. Allan Donald   d. Jacques Kallis

5. Who scored 141 runs and took 4 for 38 in India's win over Australia in the 1998 Champions Trophy tournament?
a. Rahul Dravid   b. Sachin Tendulkar   c. Yuvraj Singh   d. Robin Singh

6. Which team beat the West Indies in the 1998 Champions Trophy final?
a. South Africa   b. Australia   c. England   d. India

7. Which West Indian batsman scored the most runs in the 1998 Champions Trophy tournament?
a. Keith Arthurton   b. Philo Wallace   c. Brian Lara   d. Carl Hooper

8. Who was the winning South African captain in the Champions Trophy of 1998?
a. Hansie Cronje   b. Mark Boucher   c. Nicky Boje   d. Jonty Rhodes

9. Which team won their first major cricket tournament in 2000 when winning the Champions Trophy?
a. Pakistan   b. England   c. Sri Lanka   d. New Zealand

10. How many teams took part in the 2000 Champions Trophy?
a. 8   b. 11   c. 16   d. 20

11. When is the next Champions Trophy tournament scheduled to take place?
a. 2023   b. 2025   c. 2027   d. 2029

12. Who took the player of the match award in the 2000 Champions Trophy final by scoring a century?
a. Scott Styris   b. Stephen Fleming   c. Chris Cairns   d. Nathan Astle

13. Which non-test playing nation hosted the 2000 Champions Trophy tournament?
a. UAE   b. Netherlands   c. Kenya   d. Canada

14. Where was the 2002 Champions Trophy tournament originally due to be held before being changed to Sri Lanka?
a. Pakistan   b. West Indies   c. India   d. England

15. Which team made its debut in the 2002 Champions Trophy tournament?
a. Netherlands   b. Kenya   c. UAE   d. Oman

16. What was the result in the 2002 Champions Trophy final?
a. India win   b. Sri Lanka win   c. No result   d. Tied

17. Which Indian batsman was the top run-scorer in the 2002 Champions Trophy competition?
a. Rahul Dravid   b. Yuvraj Singh   c. Sachin Tendulkar   d. Virender Sehwag

18. London, Birmingham and Cardiff were the hosts in which year of the Champions Trophy?
a. 2010   b. 2013   c. 2017   d. 2021

19. How many times have England won the Champions Trophy title?
a. None   b. Once   c. Twice   d. Three times

20. India beat which host nation in the 2013 Champions Trophy final?
a. West Indies   b. Australia   c. England   d. Pakistan

21. Who was the Man of the Tournament in the 2013 Champions Trophy event?
a. Virat Kohli   b. Chris Gayle   c. Shikhar Dhawan   d. Ravindra Jadeja

22. Which Australian batsman scored 135 runs off 98 balls in a 2013 Champions Trophy game?
a. Shane Watson   b. Adam Voges   c. George Bailey   d. Michael Clarke

23. Apart from India, which team has won the Champions Trophy tournament two times?
a. England   b. West Indies   c. Australia   d. Pakistan

24. Apart from the Netherlands, which other team has only appeared once in the Champions Trophy competition?
a. United States   b. Canada   c. Kenya   d. Afghanistan

25. What is England's best performance in the Champions Trophy event?
a. Winners   b. Runners-up   c. Semi-Finalists   d. Quarter-Finalists

26. Which Indian batsman has the highest average in the history of the Champions Trophy with 88.16?
a. Rohit Sharma   b. Virender Sehwag   c. Sachin Tendulkar   d. Virat Kohli

27. Which Sri Lankan player has the best bowling figures of 6 for 14 in the Champions Trophy tournament?
a. Farveez Maharoof   b. Lasith Malinga
c. Chaminda Vaas   d. Muttiah Muralitharan

28. Which West Indian bowler took the first ever hat-trick in the 2006 Champions Trophy event?
a. Dwayne Bravo   b. Fidel Edwards   c. Jerome Taylor   d. Dwayne Smith

29. Which team has recorded the highest total in the history of the Champions Trophy?
a. Pakistan   b. Australia   c. India   d. New Zealand

30. Which team has recorded the lowest total in the Champions Trophy event?
a. United States   b. Kenya   c. Zimbabwe   d. Bangladesh

TWENTY20 WORLD CUP

1. In which year was the first Twenty20 World Cup held?
a. 2007   b. 2006   c. 2005   d. 2008

2. Which is the only team to have won the World Twenty20 Cup twice?
a. Australia   b. Pakistan   c. India   d. West Indies

3. At which ground was the first final of the World Twenty20 Cup held?
a. Johannesburg   b. Durban   c. Cape Town   d. Centurion

4. Which team won the inaugural Twenty20 World Cup tournament by beating Pakistan in the final?
a. England   b. Australia   c. New Zealand   d. India

5. Who were the most recent winners of the Twenty20 World Cup competition in 2021?
a. Australia   b. India   c. England   d. New Zealand

6. Which team have been runners-up twice in the Twenty20 World Cup tournament?
a. England   b. West Indies   c. Pakistan   d. Sri Lanka

7. Which two teams made their debuts at the Twenty20 World Cup in 2021?
a. UAE & USA   b. Kenya & Ireland
c. Oman & Bhutan   d. Namibia & Papua New Guinea

8. In the 2007 Twenty20 World Cup, what was the next stage called after the group stages were completed?
a. Super 8s   b. Quarter-Finals   c. Super 12   d. Super 10

9. What two major feats did Indian batsman Yuvraj Singh record in a 2007 Twenty20 World Cup game?
a. Fastest twenty20 international 50 & 6 sixes in an over   b. Fastest 50 & fastest 100
c. 6 fours & 6 sixes in an over   d. 6 sixes & fastest 100

10. Who was the suffering bowler when Yuvraj Singh hit six sixes in an over at the 2007 Twenty20 World Cup?
a. Paul Collingwood   b. James Anderson   c. Stuart Broad   d. Chris Tremlett

11. By how many runs did India beat Australia by in the semi-finals of the 2007 Twenty20 World Cup?
a. 1 run   b. 5 runs   c. 15 runs   d. 50 runs

12. Who took the winning wicket in the 2007 World Twenty20 final?
a. S. Sreesanth   b. Harbhajan Singh   c. Joginder Sharma   d. Irfan Pathan

13. What caused the abandonment of the 2020 World Twenty20 competition?
a. Flu pandemic   b. Covid-19 virus   c. General Election   d. Bad weather

14. Where was the 2021 Twenty20 World Cup event moved to?
a. West Indies to Pakistan to England   b. Australia to India to UAE/Oman
c. Sri Lanka to Pakistan to New Zealand   d. Kenya to Ireland to Scotland

15. Who was the player of the match in the 2021 Twenty20 World Cup final?
a. Steve Smith   b. Marnus Labuschagne   c. Trent Boult   d. Mitchell Marsh

16. Who scored the most runs in the Twenty20 World Cup event in 2021?
a. Jos Buttler   b. Rohit Sharma   c. Babar Azam   d. Ross Taylor

17. Which former Australian batsman was one of the match referees in the 2021 World Twenty20 tournament?
a. David Boon   b. Ricky Ponting   c. Tom Moody   d. Mark Taylor

18. How many grounds were used for the 2021 World Twenty20 tournament?
a. One   b. Four   c. Nine   d. Eleven

19. Who won the 2016 Twenty20 World Cup event?
a. England   b. Pakistan   c. Sri Lanka   d. West Indies

20. Who was defeated in the 2016 Twenty20 World Cup final?
a. England   b. Australia   c. Pakistan   d. New Zealand

21. Which Indian batsman was player of the tournament in the 2016 Twenty20 World Cup?
a. KL Rahul   b. Rohit Sharma   c. Virat Kohli   d. Shreyas Iyer

22. Which England bowler took the most wickets for his country in the 2016 Twenty20 World Cup tournament?
a. David Willey   b. Adil Rashid   c. Chris Jordan   d. Ben Stokes

23. At which Twenty20 tournament did Afghanistan make their debut?
a. 2000   b. 2005   c. 2010   d. 2015

24. How many games did Afghanistan win in their first Twenty20 World Cup tournament?
a. Two   b. Three   c. None   d. Five

25. Who led Australia to victory in the 2010 Twenty20 World Cup semi-final with a brilliant 60 not out off 24 balls batting at number 7?
a. Adam Gilchrist   b. Damien Martyn   c. Matthew Hayden   d. Michael Hussey

26. Which broadcaster showed the 2010 Twenty20 World Cup competition in the UK?
a. Virgin   b. Sky Sports   c. BT Sport   d. ESPN

27. Which team has played the most matches and also won the most games in the history of the Twenty20 World Cup competition?
a. England   b. Australia   c. Sri Lanka   d. India

28. The highest Twenty20 World Cup total of 260-6 was scored by which team?
a. Sri Lanka   b. Pakistan   c. New Zealand   d. West Indies

29. By how many runs did Sri Lanka beat Kenya by when totalling 260-6 in a Twenty20 World Cup match in 2007?
a. 72   b. 132   c. 172   d. 222

30. Which team has scored the two lowest totals in the history of the Twenty20 World Cup?
a. Netherlands   b. Ireland   c. Afghanistan   d. Kenya

31. Who did this team face on both occasions when totalling the two lowest scores in the history of the Twenty20 World Cup?
a. Sri Lanka   b. India   c. West Indies   d. Australia

32. Which Sri Lankan batsman is the only player to have scored over a 1000 runs in the Twenty20 World Cup competition history?
a. Sanath Jayasuriya   b. Kumar Sangakkara
c. Angelo Mathews   d. Mahela Jayawardene

33. How many centuries has Mahela Jayawardene hit in the Twenty20 World Cup competition?
a. None   b. One   c. Four   d. Seven

34. Which England batsman blasted 116 off 64 balls in a 2014 Twenty20 World Cup match against Sri Lanka?
a. Jos Buttler   b. Ben Stokes   c. Alex Hales   d. David Willey

35. Who has the highest average in the history of the Twenty20 World Cup – a remarkable 76.81 in 19 innings?
a. Joe Root   b. David Warner   c. Babar Azam   d. Virat Kohli

36. What other record does Virat Kohli hold in the Twenty20 World Cup event?
a. Most centuries   b. Most sixes   c. Most boundaries   d. Most 50+ scores

37. One player holds the records for both the fastest 100 and the most sixes in the history of the Twenty20 World Cup competition. Can you name him?
a. Andre Russell   b. Kieron Pollard   c. Chris Gayle   d. Ben Stokes

38. Which Bangladeshi bowler has taken the most wickets in Twenty20 World Cup history?
a. Shakib Al Hasan   b. Mahedi Hasan   c. Abdur Razzak   d. Mashrafe Mortaza

39. Who attained the remarkable figures of 6 for 8 playing against Zimbabwe in a Twenty20 World Cup game?
a. Rangana Herath   b. Muttiah Muralitharan
c. Ravichandran Ashwin   d. Ajantha Mendis

40. Which speedster achieved the first ever hat-trick in the 2007 Twenty20 World Cup tournament?
a. Brett Lee   b. Morne Morkel   c. Fidel Edwards   d. Shane Bond

GUESS THE PLAYER

1. I was born in the 1840s, had two brothers that also played cricket, was a doctor, had a long beard, and was prone to 'bend the rules'. Who am I?
a. Billy Murdoch   b. Alfred Mynn   c. WG Grace   d. Tom Emmett

2. I was a Yorkshireman who was born in the 1910s and died in 1990. I was an opening batsman for England, once held the record test score, scored over 40,000 runs and averaged over 55 in his career. Who am I?
a. Len Hutton   b. Jack Hobbs   c. Wally Hammond   d. Herbert Sutcliffe

3. I was an Australian batsman with a career average of over 95, nearly 100 in tests, 29 test hundreds, a top score of 452 not out, most test double hundreds, 117 career centuries, and numerous other batting records. I am famous for practising with a golf ball when I was younger. Who am I?
a. Stan McCabe   b. Bill Ponsford   c. Bill Woodfull   d. Don Bradman

4. I was an opener who held the record for the most test runs and centuries, had a top score of 340, an average of 65 against the West Indies, once scored 36 in a full one-day innings at the World Cup, and is now a television commentator. Who am I?
a. Sunil Gavaskar   b. Sanjay Manjrekar   c. Dilip Vengsarkar   d. Ravi Shastri

5. I was born in the 1940s, was partly named after the singer Bob Dylan, took a match-winning 8-43 against the Australians, played for Warwickshire, once held the record for most test wickets by an English bowler, and became a Sky TV commentator. Who am I?
a. Ian Botham   b. Mike Hendrick   c. Chris Old   d. Bob Willis

6. I once held the test wicket-taking record, formed a great wicket taking partnership with wicket-keeper Rodney Marsh, became a bowling coach in India, and once used an aluminium bat! Who am I?
a. Jeff Thomson   b. Dennis Lillee   c. Richie Benaud   d. Rodney Hogg

7. I made my test debut aged 19, was the youngest player to score a 200 in tests, scored six double centuries in tests, parents once lived in India, coached the Pakistan cricket team, and once swung a bat at Dennis Lillee! Who am I?
a. Javed Miandad   b. Mudassar Nazar   c. Imran Khan   d. Zaheer Abbas

8. I captained Pakistan to World Cup victory in 1992, played county cricket for Sussex, attended Oxford University, was a key exponent of the reverse swing, helped build a cancer hospital in Pakistan, and am now the Prime Minister of that country. Who am I?
a. Sarfraz Nawaz   b. Wasim Akram   c. Imran Khan   d. Mushtaq Mohammad

9. I scored a triple century against India, helped modernise one-day cricket, scored over 10000 runs in one-day internationals, helped the team to win the 1996 World Cup, and was once a politician serving in Sri Lanka. Who am I?
a. Arjuna Ranatunga   b. Aravinda de Silva
c. Roshan Mahanama   d. Sanath Jayasuriya

10. I was born in 1971, took over 370 test and 400 ODI wickets, once lived in Sharjah, bowled leg-spin at school, was an expert at the in-swinging yorker, and now coach and commentate. Who am I?
a. Wasim Akram   b. Waqar Younis   c. Imran Khan   d. Shahid Afridi

11. I was involved in a 664-run partnership playing for my school, only player to score 100 international centuries, I have over 30000 international runs, a first class average of over 57, a former member of parliament, and, after Bradman, probably the most prolific run-getter of all time. Who am I?
a. Sachin Tendulkar   b. Rahul Dravid   c. Sunil Gavaskar   d. Sourav Ganguly

12. I have over 300 test wickets, played county cricket for Somerset, took five wickets on my test debut, played football for Scunthorpe United, held the world record for the most test wickets, did numerous charity walks and have recently been awarded a Knighthood. Who am I?
a. Bob Willis   b. Ian Botham   c. Fred Trueman   d. Derek Underwood

13. I am a leg-spin bowler, made my test debut in 2018, have competed in many Twenty20 competitions, was born in Afghanistan and was the youngest international captain named twenty20 international player of the decade in 2020. Who am I?
a. Imran Tahir   b. Rashid Khan   c. Mohammad Nabi   d. Asghar Afghan

14. I was born in Pakistan but I play for South Africa. I am a right-arm leg spinner with a bowling average of 15 in twenty20 internationals and I am their country's most successful spin bowler. Who am I?
a. Nicky Boje   b. Keshav Maharaj   c. Imran Tahir   d. Paul Adams

15. I am a fast bowler from Yorkshire, first bowler to take 300 test wickets, a commentator, presented sports tv show Indoor League, liked to smoke a pipe, and was nicknamed 'Fiery'. Who am I?
a. Fred Trueman   b. Alec Bedser   c. Brian Statham   d. Ken Higgs

16. I am the undefeated captain of Australia, over 6 foot tall and weighing 21 stone/294 lbs, briefly played Aussie Rules football, and nicknamed the 'Big Ship'. Who am I?
a. Charles Macartney   b. Clarrie Grimmett   c. Warwick Armstrong   d. David Boon

17. I captained in three successful Ashes series, played 156 tests, over 10000 runs, captained Australia to victory in the 1987 World Cup, and am often referred to as 'Captain Grumpy'. Who am I?
a. Kim Hughes   b. Graham Yallop   c. Steve Waugh   d. Allan Border

18. I am the first South African to take 300 test wickets, born in Bloemfontein, played for Warwickshire, now a coach, and nicknamed 'White Lightning'. Who am I?
a. Shaun Pollock   b. Allan Donald   c. Lance Klusener   d. Fanie de Villiers

19. I have two triple hundreds in tests, record sixes hitter, numerous twenty20 cricket records, fastest scoring records, and known as the 'Universe Boss'. Who am I?
a. Chris Gayle   b. Carl Hooper   c. Andre Russell   d. Dwayne Bravo

20. I formed a formidable opening partnership with Desmond Haynes, scored two double hundreds against England in 1984, played for Hampshire, and held numerous highest score one-day records. Who am I?
a. Desmond Haynes   b. Roy Fredericks   c. Gordon Greenidge   d. Clive Lloyd

ENGLAND CRICKET

1. Who once scored 333 for England in a test match?
a. Geoff Boycott   b. David Gower   c. Denis Compton   d. Graham Gooch

2. Who were the opponents when this player scored 333 in a test match in 1990?
a. Australia   b. Pakistan   c. West Indies   d. India

3. On which ground did this player score 333 in a test innings?
a. The Oval   b. Lord's   c. Headingley   d. Edgbaston

4. When did England play their first ever test match?
a. 1827   b. 1877   c. 1843   d. 1861

5. What was the result when England played their first ever test match?
a. Loss to Australia by 45 runs   b. Loss to South Africa by 45 runs
c. A win by 45 runs   d. Draw

6. Which player has scored the most test runs for England?
a. Colin Cowdrey   b. Geoff Boycott   c. Graham Gooch   d. Alastair Cook

7. Who has taken the most wickets for England in tests?
a. Derek Underwood   b. Ian Botham   c. Stuart Broad   d. James Anderson

8. Which batsman has scored the most test centuries for England?
a. Wally Hammond   b. Alastair Cook   c. Michael Vaughan   d. Andrew Strauss

9. Which opener scored his 100th century in a test match in 1977?
a. John Edrich   b. Mike Denness   c. Geoff Boycott   d. Colin Cowdrey

10. How many times have England beaten Scotland in a test match?
a. Never   b. Twice   c. Four times   d. Nine times

11. How many times have England won the World Cup?
a. Twice   b. Four times   c. Once   d. Six times

12. Who did England lose to in the 1979 World Cup final?
a. Australia   b. New Zealand   c. West Indies   d. Pakistan

13. In which year did England win the World Twenty20 competition?
a. 2010   b. 2012   c. 2015   d. 2021

14. Have England ever won the Champions Trophy?
a. Yes – once   b. Yes – twice   c. No   d. Yes – four times

15. What was the overseas touring England team called by in the early days of test cricket?
a. Etonians   b. ICC   c. MCC   d. MCCC

16. How many different test match grounds have England used?
a. 9   b. 12   c. 16   d. 20

17. Which player bowled the first ball in test cricket for England?
a. Tom Emmett   b. George Ulyett   c. Alfred Shaw   d. Harry Jupp

18. Which batsman faced the first ball and also scored the first run for England in test match cricket?
a. John Selby   b. George Ulyett   c. James Lillywhite   d. Harry Jupp

19. Who scored England's first test century?
a. WG Grace   b. Harry Jupp   c. Edward Grace   d. Lord Harris

20. Who scored England's first double century in tests?
a. WG Grace   b. Wally Hammond   c. Reg 'Tip' Foster   d. Jack Hobbs

21. What record total did England achieve in a 1928 test match against Australia?
a. 432   b. 518   c. 636   d. 701

22. What record test score did England's Wally Hammond accomplish in 1933?
a. 136   b. 236   c. 336   d. 366

23. What test batting record did Wally Hammond achieve during his monster innings in 1933 against New Zealand?
a. Fastest 50   b. Fastest 100   c. Fastest 200   d. Fastest 300

24. Who broke Don Bradman's test record score in 1938?
a. Joe Hardstaff   b. Wally Hammond   c. Len Hutton   d. Arthur Fagg

25. Which English bowler took 49 wickets in only four tests against South Africa?
a. Jim Laker   b. Johnny Briggs   c. Fred Trueman   d. Sydney Barnes

26. For how much did England bowl out India for in a 1974 test match?
a. 22   b. 42   c. 82   d. 122

27. On which team did England inflict the lowest total on in test cricket?
a. Pakistan   b. West Indies   c. New Zealand   d. South Africa

28. How many county cricket teams are there in England and Wales?
a. 12   b. 14   c. 16   d. 18

29. Who is England's most successful spin bowler in tests?
a. Derek Underwood   b. Jim Laker   c. Graeme Swann   d. John Emburey

30. Which fast bowler currently holds the world test wickets record?
a. Ian Botham   b. Steve Harmison   c. Stuart Broad   d. James Anderson

31. Who has scored the most test fifties for England?
a. Alastair Cook   b. Geoff Boycott   c. Graham Gooch   d. Andrew Strauss

32. Which England bowler took 7 for 12 against the West Indies in a test match?
a. James Anderson   b. Matthew Hoggard   c. Graeme Swann   d. Steve Harmison

33. How many times did England lose to the West Indies in the 1984 and 1985/86 test series combined?
a. 8   b. 10   c. 12   d. 14

34. When did England last win an Ashes series?
a. 2005   b. 2010   c. 2015   d. 2020

35. With whom do England play for the Wisden Trophy?
a. India   b. Australia   c. West Indies   d. South Africa

36. How many times have England lost to Zimbabwe in tests?
a. Never   b. Once   c. Three times   d. Eight times

37. For the loss of only one wicket, how many runs did England score against Australia at Brisbane in the 2010/11 test series?
a. 545   b. 463   c. 490   d. 517

38. Which England captain scored over 700 runs in the test series win over the Australians in 1985?
a. Mike Gatting   b. Tim Robinson   c. David Gower   d. Graham Gooch

39. Who was England's most successful bowler in the 1985 Ashes series?
a. John Emburey   b. Ian Botham   c. Phil Edmonds   d. Richard Ellison

40. Who smashed 258 runs off only 198 balls in a test match in South Africa in 2016?
a. Jonny Bairstow   b. Alex Hales   c. Joe Root   d. Ben Stokes

41. Who recently scored the most test runs in the 2021 calendar year?
a. Rory Burns   b. Zak Crawley   c. Joe Root   d. Ben Stokes

42. How many wickets did Yorkshire-born Wilfred Rhodes take in his impressive career?
a. 1845   b. 3045   c. 4204   d. 5799

43. When was the last time England lost a home test series?
a. 2018   b. 2019   c. 2020   d. 2021

44. When was the last time West Indies beat England in a test series?
a. 2013   b. 2015   c. 2017   d. 2019

45. Who currently holds the record for the highest individual score by an English batsman in a one-day international game?
a. David Gower   b. Allan Lamb   c. Jos Buttler   d. Jason Roy

46. Who holds the best bowling record in ODI matches for England?
a. Andrew Flintoff   b. Vic Marks   c. Paul Collingwood   d. Chris Jordan

47. When are England due to play Afghanistan in a test match?
a. 2022   b. 2024   c. 2026   d. No schedule

48. Who became England captain in the 1981 test series after Ian Botham was dismissed from the role?
a. Graham Gooch   b. David Gower   c. Mike Brearley   d. Geoff Boycott

49. Who is England's most successful test captain with 27 wins?
a. Michael Vaughan   b. Andrew Strauss   c. Mike Gatting   d. Joe Root

50. Where are England currently in the World Test Championship table?
a. Ninth   b. Second   c. Third   d. Fifth

GENERAL KNOWLEDGE

1. What was the record test partnership between Javed Miandad and Mudassar Nazar against India in 1983?
a. 251   b. 351   c. 451   d. 551

2. Whose record did Javed Miandad and Mudassar Nazar equal when compiling a partnership of 451 against India in 1983?
a. Don Bradman & Bill Ponsford   b. Jack Hobbs & Herbert Sutcliffe
c. Sunil Gavaskar & Gundappa Viswanath   c. Conrad Hunte & Gary Sobers

3. What are the two triple century scores recorded by West Indian Chris Gayle in test matches?
a. 317 & 333   b. 301 & 324   c. 316 & 317   d. 302 & 329

4. How many tests did Australian Steve Waugh play?
a. 95   b. 168   c. 125   d. 145

5. How many runs did Steve Waugh score before being dismissed for the first time by Angus Fraser in the 1989 Ashes test series?
a. 293   b. 393   c. 429   d. 364

6. Which organisation has Australian player Steve Waugh supported in India?
a. Children's hospital   b. Cancer hospital   c. Leper Colony   d. UNICEF

7. Why did England's Andrew Flintoff retire from cricket?
a. Finger injury   b. Back injury   c. Knee problems   d. Head injury

8. Who was the first Sri Lankan batsman to score a hundred in tests?
a. Arjuna Ranatunga   b. Sidath Wettimuny   c. Asanka Gurusinha   d. Roy Dias

9. After Australia and England, who became the third team to play test cricket?
a. West Indies   b. South Africa   c. New Zealand   d. India

10. Which is the only team to have won their first ever test match?
a. England   b. Pakistan   c. Australia   d. West Indies

11. How many matches did it take for England to win their first test?
a. 5   b. 2   c. 9   d. 12

12. When did India enter the test match arena?
a. 1922   b. 1932   c. 1942   d. 1952

13. In which year did the West Indies play their first test?
a. 1912   b. 1922   c. 1928   d. 1932

14. How many matches did it take Pakistan to win their first test match?
a. One   b. Two   c. Three   d. Four

15. What promising position were Sri Lanka in before losing their inaugural test to England in 1982?
a. 107 ahead in their second innings with seven wickets remaining
b. 162 ahead in their second innings with seven wickets remaining
c. 200 run lead on first innings
d. 92 ahead in their second innings with nine wickets remaining

16. Which English side has won the county championship on the most occasions?
a. Surrey   b. Middlesex   c. Yorkshire   d. Lancashire

17. Which team won the English championship title in 2021?
a. Kent   b. Essex   c. Sussex   d. Warwickshire

18. The Oval is home to which club?
a. Warwickshire   b. Glamorgan   c. Surrey   d. Derbyshire

19. Who play the majority of their games at Edgbaston, Birmingham?
a. Middlesex   b. Leicestershire   c. Nottinghamshire   d. Warwickshire

20. Who are the current sponsors of The Oval cricket ground?
a. Toyota   b. Specsavers   c. Prudential   d. Kia

21. When was the last time Yorkshire won the county championship?
a. 2012   b. 2013   c. 2014   d. 2015

22. Which Indian team has won the most Ranji Trophy titles?
a. Mumbai   b. Karnataka   c. Vidarbha   d. Delhi

23. Tamil Nadu are the most successful team in the Syed Mushtaq Ali twenty20 competition. How many titles ahve they won?
a. Three   b. Five   c. Seven   d. Nine

24. Which player had an average of 67 in Indian first-class cricket but never played test cricket?
a. Amol Muzumdar   b. Sanjay Manjrekar   c. Ajay Sharma   d. Raman Lamba

25. When did Indian batsman Sachin Tendulkar play his first Ranji Trophy game?
a. 1985   b. 1988   c. 1995   d. 1997

26. Don Bradman scored how many runs, and at what average, in Australia's first-class state competition?
a. 6345 & 95   b. 5987 & 85   c. 7257 & 98   d. 8926 & 110

27. Which Australian player has scored two quadruple hundreds in first-class cricket?
a. Don Bradman   b. Stan McCabe   c. Bill Woodfull   d. Bill Ponsford

28. What were the two individual scores by this player when compiling his two quadruple centuries?
a. 401 & 433   b. 422 & 433   c. 401 & 429   d. 429 & 437

29. When was the first first-class match played in Sri Lanka?
a. 1916   b. 1926   c. 1936   d. 1946

30. Which Sri Lankan bowler was the first to take 300 test wickets?
a. Chaminda Vaas   b. Asantha de Mel   c. Muttiah Muralitharan   d. Lasith Malinga

31. What record number of test wickets did New Zealand bowler Richard Hadlee take?
a. 331 test wickets   b. 371 test wickets   c. 431 test wickets   d. 471 test wickets

32. Who eventually broke Richard Hadlee's test wicket-taking record?
a. Kapil Dev   b. Shane Warne   c. Muttiah Muralitharan   d. Courtney Walsh

33. Which team has won the most titles in New Zealand's first-class domestic cricket competition?
a. Auckland   b. Canterbury   c. Otago   d. Central Districts

34. How many times did Pakistan bowler Fazal Mahmood take ten wickets in a test match?
a. Once   b. Twice   c. Four times   d. Six times

35. How many matches did Pakistani fast bowler Fazal Mahmood play for his team?
a. 14   b. 24   c. 34   d. 54

36. Who is the only Pakistani batsman to have scored over a 100 hundreds in first-class cricket?
a. Hanif Mohammad   b. Zaheer Abbas   c. Javed Miandad   d. Inzamam-ul-Haq

37. Who was the first player in history to achieve the feat of 100 first-class centuries?
a. Jack Hobbs   b. WG Grace   c. Herbert Sutcliffe   d. Tom Hayward

38. What is the name of West Indies' first-class cricket competition?
a. Shell Cup   b. Busta Cup   c. Regional Four Day Competition   d. Shell Shield

39. Which side has been the most successful in the West Indian first-class cricket competition?
a. Jamaica   b. Barbados   c. Leeward Islands   d. Trinidad & Tobago

40. When did the South African first-class teams change their names to mainly one word titles for their domestic competitions?
a. 1997   b. 2000   c. 2004   d. 2007

41. With which letter do the majority of the Zimbabwean first-class teams begin with?
a. S   b. T   c. N   d. M

42. When did Ireland enter the test match arena?
a. 2014   b. 2016   c. 2018   d. 2020

43. Who did Ireland play in their first ever test match?
a. England   b. India   c. Pakistan   d. Bangladesh

44. What was the result of that game?
a. Pakistan win by 108 runs   b. Pakistan win by 2 wickets
c. Ireland win by 24 runs   d. Pakistan win by 5 wickets

45. What is the highest team total in first-class cricket?
a. 900   b. 951   c. 1107   d. 1345

46. Which team have that record?
a. Victoria   b. Australia   c. India   d. New South Wales

47. Which team have drawn the most number of test matches?
a. Pakistan   b. West Indies   c. England   d. Australia

48. When the 1960 test at Brisbane ended in the first ever tied result, which two teams were taking part?
a. England & South Africa   b. England & Australia
c. Australia & West Indies   d. West Indies & New Zealand

49. Which are the only two other teams to have been involved in a similar tied result in a test match in 1986?
a. India & England   b. Pakistan & West Indies
c. Sri Lanka & New Zealand   d. Australia & India

50. What target was the batting side chasing in that game?
a. 234   b. 347   c. 374   d. 434

ANAGRAM ROUND

The following 30 anagrams are the first and surname of famous cricketers.
How many can you get?

1. Adda bland norm

2. Auckland hinters

3. Airbeds folgers

4. Armin hank

5. Ahab timon

6. Ann whereas

7. Aviv chris dr

8. Albania rr

9. Alli jess quack

10. Him nods

11. Karma swami

12. Avior hitkl

13. Deann majoress

14. Carlos taikoa

15. Ahriman tatar thulium

16. Agana markka rusk

17. Elk vapid

18. Aldrich adhere

19. Aldrich stigma

20. Archy legis

21. Can length mgr

22. Corty kingpin

23. Gustav hewe

24. Adar div hurl

25. Lusaka ravings

26. Abator shaikh

27. Aborter muscly

28. Aaren headway jamel

29. Ad tensely

30. Dall ladonna

ANSWERS

WORLD CUP

1. Australia
2. Sachin Tendulkar
3. Glenn McGrath
4. South Africa, Zimbabwe and Kenya
5. Australia & New Zealand
6. India
7. Kane Williamson
8. One
9. Five
10. 1992
11. Ricky Ponting
12. Canada
13. 417
14. Australia
15. 2007
16. 1996
17. 2007
18. MS Dhoni
19. Sachin Tendulkar
20. Martin Guptill
21. West Indies
22. 4
23. 20
24. Australia
25. Kenya - semi finals
26. Sri Lanka
27. Dickie Bird
28. Gary Gilmour
29. 60
30. 21 runs off 1 ball
31. Gaddafi Stadium, Lahore, Pakistan
32. None
33. 152
34. Six sixes in an over
35. 338
36. 413-5
37. 397-6
38. 349
39. Clive Lloyd and Viv Richards
40. 100 mph
41. Ben Stokes
42. 53
43. It required a super over
44. 241
45. over 93,000
46. 138
47. Kumar Sangakkara
48. Australia
49. East Africa
50. 56.95
51. Three consecutive ducks
52. 372
53. One-handed diving catch
54. Old Trafford
55. Glenn McGrath
56. Andy Roberts
57. 116
58. 1973
59. 36 all out
60. Dennis Amiss
61. Sunil Gavaskar
62. East Africa
63. 17
64. Ricky Ponting
65. 237 not out
66. 714

67. Kevin O'Brien
68. Brendon McCullum
69. Prudential
70. Chris Gayle
71. Steve Bucknor
72. Javed Miandad and Sachin Tendulkar
73. Represented two countries
74. Nolan Clarke (Netherlands)
75. Ireland
76. 115
77. Most fifties
78. 1996
79. Graham Gooch
80. Chetan Sharma

CRICKET TERMINOLOGY

1. Bounces zero times before reaching the batsman
2. Leg before wicket
3. Ten
4. Australia
5. Leg-spinner
6. 2001
7. 2005
8. MCC
9. 111
10. Yes - by being run out
11. Scoring zero in both innings
12. Mike Gatting
13. Ball
14. Abdominal region
15. Boundary
16. Toes
17. Between mid-on and mid-off
18. Twelfth man
19. Cricket Max
20. Fielding position

STADIUMS

1. Narendra Modi Stadium, Ahmedabad, India
2. Melbourne Cricket Ground, Melbourne, Australia
3. Eden Gardens, Kolkata
4. Australia and India
5. The Oval
6. 121
7. Sophia Gardens, Cardiff
8. South Africa
9. UAE
10. New York
11. India
12. Mumbai, India
13. Melbourne, Australia
14. R. Premadasa Stadium, Colombo
15. St. John's, Antigua
16. Australia
17. Docklands, Melbourne
18. Harare and Bulawayo
19. Grace Road
20. Middlesex

ICC WORLD TEST CHAMPIONSHIP

1. All eligible test playing nations
2. 2013
3. New Zealand
4. India
5. Marnus Labuschagne
6. David Warner
7. India
8. Ajaz Patel
9. Rose Bowl
10. ICC Champions Trophy
11. Martin Crowe
12. Ten
13. ICC Champions Trophy
14. The Ashes
15. Edgbaston, Birmingham
16. Tied
17. India
18. Afghanistan, Ireland and Zimbabwe
19. Ravichandran Ashwin
20. Reserve day used
21. Best-of-three series
22. 1.6 million US dollars
23. Bangladesh
24. 2021-23
25. 12
26. Joe Root (England)
27. International Cricket Council
28. Fourth
29. Stuart Broad
30. England

IPL

1. 2008
2. Indian Premier League
3. Rajasthan Royals
4. Brendon McCullum
5. Rajasthan Royals
6. Sohail Tanvir
7. Mumbai Indians
8. Chennai Super Kings
9. Kolkata Knight Riders
10. Virat Kohli
11. Royal Challengers Bangalore
12. David Warner
13. KL Rahul
14. Chris Gayle
15. AB de Villiers
16. Chris Gayle
17. 175 not out
18. Lasith Malinga
19. Alzarri Joseph
20. Three
21. Dwayne Bravo
22. Mahendra Singh Dhoni & Dinesh Karthik
23. Suresh Raina
24. AB de Villiers & Virat Kohli
25. MS Dhoni
26. Deccan Chargers
27. Twice
28. Royal Challengers Bangalore, Delhi Capitals & Punjab Kings
29. UAE & South Africa
30. Chennai Super Kings
31. Awarded to the player with most runs
32. Awarded to the player with most wickets
33. Bhuvneshwar Kumar
34. 2010
35. None
36. Rishabh Pant
37. 2009
38. Chennai Super Kings
39. No - never
40. Mumbai Indians
41. Chennai Super Kings
42. 11 times
43. Rajasthan Royals
44. Royal Challengers Bangalore
45. Lowest team total
46. David Warner
47. KL Rahul
48. Chris Gayle
49. Chris Morris
50. Lungi Ngidi
51. Sunil Narine
52. Basil Thampi
53. Lakshmipathy Balaji
54. Amit Mishra
55. Harshal Patel
56. MS Dhoni
57. Mohammad Nabi
58. Kolkata Knight Riders
59. AB de Villiers
60. Harbhajan Singh & Jagadeesha Suchith
61. Sundaram Ravi
62. Kumar Dharmasena
63. Kolkata Knight Riders

64. Preity Zinta
65. Anil Kumble
66. Mahela Jayawardene
67. S Sreesanth
68. 2010
69. Spot-fixing
70. September 2021
71. Two
72. Alcohol
73. Kolkata Knight Riders
74. Being capital of India
75. Sunrisers
76. One
77. Eight
78. Mumbai Indians
79. Rising Pune Supergiants
80. Chennai Super Kings

THE ASHES

1. Australia & England
2. 1870s
3. Charles Bannerman
4. Harry Jupp
5. A burnt bail
6. James Lillywhite
7. 19
8. 8
9. 4-0
10. Unbeaten on tour
11. 89.78
12. Wally Hammond
13. Lord's Cricket Ground
14. 340
15. Australia
16. 1882/83
17. Fred Spofforth
18. The Ashes Trophy
19. Chris Broad
20. Bill Athey
21. Mike Gatting
22. Allan Border
23. Headingley
24. Edgbaston
25. Dennis Lillee
26. Rod Marsh
27. Douglas Jardine
28. Don Bradman
29. Harold Larwood
30. Australia
31. 103
32. 334
33. Len Hutton
34. 364
35. Over 13 hours
36. 149
37. Allan Border
38. Mark
39. 839
40. Craig McDermott
41. Terry Alderman
42. Bob Willis
43. Travis Head
44. 5-1 series win
45. 0
46. Andrew Flintoff
47. Michael Kasprowicz
48. Melbourne
49. Australia 2-1
50. Double-hundred on debut
51. Highest individual score in tests
52. 656 & 611
53. Bobby Simpson
54. Ken Barrington
55. 58
56. Duck
57. 50
58. Elton John
59. David Gower
60. Vodafone
61. Npower
62. Jim Laker
63. 19
64. 20 years

65. Alec Bedser
66. Len Hutton
67. Three times
68. 2015
69. Sydney
70. 180
71. Glamorgan
72. 57
73. 727
74. 762 minutes
75. 24
76. Duncan Fletcher
77. Don Bradman
78. Jim Laker
79. Ian Botham
80. Dickie Bird

CHAMPIONS TROPHY

1. 50 overs
2. 1998
3. Bangladesh
4. Jacques Kallis
5. Sachin Tendulkar
6. South Africa
7. Philo Wallace
8. Hansie Cronje
9. New Zealand
10. 11
11. 2025
12. Chris Cairns
13. Kenya
14. India
15. Netherlands
16. No result
17. Virender Sehwag
18. 2013
19. None
20. England
21. Shikhar Dhawan
22. Shane Watson
23. Australia
24. United States
25. Runners-up
26. Virat Kohli
27. Farveez Maharoof
28. Jerome Taylor
29. New Zealand
30. United States

TWENTY20 WORLD CUP

1. 2007
2. West Indies
3. Johannesburg
4. India
5. Australia
6. Sri Lanka
7. Namibia & Papua New Guinea
8. Super 8s
9. Fastest twenty20 international 50 & 6 sixes in an over
10. Stuart Broad
11. 15 runs
12. Joginder Sharma
13. Covid-19 virus
14. Australia to India to UAE/Oman
15. Mitchell Marsh
16. Babar Azam
17. David Boon
18. Four
19. West Indies
20. England
21. Virat Kohli
22. David Willey
23. 2010
24. None
25. Michael Hussey
26. Sky Sports
27. Sri Lanka
28. Sri Lanka
29. 172
30. Netherlands
31. Sri Lanka
32. Mahela Jayawardene
33. One
34. Alex Hales
35. Virat Kohli
36. Most 50+ scores
37. Chris Gayle
38. Shakib Al Hasan
39. Ajantha Mendis
40. Brett Lee

GUESS THE PLAYER

1. WG Grace
2. Len Hutton
3. Don Bradman
4. Sunil Gavaskar
5. Bob Willis
6. Dennis Lillee
7. Javed Miandad
8. Imran Khan
9. Sanath Jayasuriya
10. Waqar Younis
11. Sachin Tendulkar
12. Ian Botham
13. Rashid Khan
14. Imran Tahir
15. Fred Trueman
16. Warwick Armstrong
17. Allan Border
18. Allan Donald
19. Chris Gayle
20. Gordon Greenidge

ENGLAND CRICKET

1. Graham Gooch
2. India
3. Lord's
4. 1877
5. Loss to Australia by 45 runs
6. Alastair Cook
7. James Anderson
8. Alastair Cook
9. Geoff Boycott
10. Never
11. Once
12. West Indies
13. 2010
14. No
15. MCC
16. Nine
17. Alfred Shaw
18. Harry Jupp
19. WG Grace
20. Reg 'Tip' Foster
21. 636
22. 336
23. Fastest 300
24. Len Hutton
25. Sydney Barnes
26. 42
27. New Zealand
28. 18
29. Derek Underwood
30. James Anderson
31. Alastair Cook
32. Steve Harmison
33. 10
34. 2015
35. West Indies
36. Never
37. 517
38. David Gower
39. Ian Botham
40. Ben Stokes
41. Joe Root
42. 4204
43. 2021
44. 2019
45. Jason Roy
46. Paul Collingwood
47. No schedule
48. Mike Brearley
49. Joe Root
50. Ninth

GENERAL KNOWLEDGE

1. 451
2. Don Bradman & Bill Ponsford
3. 317 & 333
4. 168
5. 393
6. Leper colony
7. Knee problems
8. Sidath Wettimuny
9. South Africa
10. Australia
11. 2
12. 1932
13. 1928
14. Two
15. 162 ahead in their second innings with seven wickets remaining
16. Yorkshire
17. Warwickshire
18. Surrey
19. Warwickshire
20. Kia
21. 2015
22. Mumbai
23. Three
24. Ajay Sharma
25. 1988
26. 8926 & 110
27. Bill Ponsford
28. 429 & 437
29. 1926
30. Chaminda Vaas
31. 431 test wickets
32. Kapil Dev
33. Auckland
34. Four times
35. 34
36. Zaheer Abbas
37. WG Grace
38. Regional Four Day Competition
39. Barbados
40. 2004
41. M
42. 2018
43. Pakistan
44. Pakistan win by 5 wickets
45. 1107
46. Victoria
47. England
48. Australia & West Indies
49. Australia & India
50. 347

ANAGRAM ROUND

1. Donald Bradman
2. Sachin Tendulkar
3. Garfield Sobers
4. Imran Khan
5. Ian Botham
6. Shane Warne
7. Viv Richards
8. Brian Lara
9. Jacques Kallis
10. MS Dhoni
11. Wasim Akram
12. Virat Kohli
13. James Anderson
14. Alastair Cook
15. Muttiah Muralitharan
16. Kumar Sangakkara
17. Kapil Dev
18. Richard Hadlee
19. Adam Gilchrist
20. Chris Gayle
21. Glenn McGrath
22. Ricky Ponting
23. Steve Waugh
24. Rahul Dravid
25. Sunil Gavaskar
26. Shoaib Akhtar
27. Curtly Ambrose
28. Mahela Jayawardene
29. Dale Steyn
30. Allan Donald

Printed in Great Britain
by Amazon